Practical
Magic

PRACTICAL MAGIC

Poems
by
Carl Bode

Swallow Press
Ohio University Press

Chicago   Athens, Ohio   London

Copyright © 1981 by Carl Bode
All rights reserved
Printed in the United States of America

Published by
The Ohio University Press

Library of Congress Cataloging in Publication Data

Bode, Carl, 1911-
   Practical Magic.
    I. Title.
PS3503.0'164P7   811'.54   80-17597
ISBN 0-8040-0362-9 clothbound
ISBN 0-8040-0373-4 paperbound

To Chad Walsh

CONTENTS

Spells and Illusions

The Conjurer's Cloaks

Spells and Illusions

THE INCANTATION

Night. No stars. Let hellgramites emerge
From the pale satin skull. Let lacewings cling
To the latticed cage of ribs while chigoes sing
Along the spine a spinal dirge.
Let gadflies or emmets dye the white pelvis black
As aphids outline all the limbs in green.
Scarabs, go rim the eyeballs till they look serene;
Sear all mortality away, spiders, with your poison-sac
And you, ephemerids, hang up a pall of cloud.
But let my love kneel down, denying I am dead
And, staring at these busy bones much comforted,
Reject the sycophantic shroud;
And let her say in accents only slightly strange
"Dear friend, I see no change, I see no change."

THE ASTRAL SHIP

I drown in the sky, clutching the handrail
While reciting the gnomes of Buddha. The

Conductor stamps my trembling ticket; his
Own hand is blue. My wife scans my face

With experienced eyes; only two tics are
Showing. I am alone.

Miles below, upon the clouds angels stomp
Silently in their snowshoes, while their

Older children ski. The youngest ones eat
Cloud and are sweetly reproved. I peer

Down on them all from the airplane, consoling
Them for their happiness. For each one wears

A heavy halo, with floating from it a ribbon
That says "I smile."

Miserable angels, I sweat with fear and pity
You. My tics jump like arboreal insects;

My stomach corrodes with anxiety. And I
Hear the motor of the plane sputter and

Then stop. Yet I breathe. And the motor
Catches again perhaps perhaps perhaps and I hug my ague
To me like a child.

NOTE FROM THE UNDERGROUND

The note begins: The Sea of Tranquility lies
At the west end of the moon, and is dry.
It looks something like the face of a wise
Eisenhower in a flat pale sky.

Dust lies deep on the sea, the note adds,
And yet over its soft surface flounder herds
Of lunar elk, shod in their great sloppy pads.
Birds? There are only the bones of birds.

Nothing moves over the worn scars of battle
Except, under billows of moon dust,
Those shuffling, platitudinous cattle.
The sole smell is a smell like ancient rust.

You or I, dropped into that powdery sea,
Could breathe but once. Yet we hurl ourselves away
From steamy teeming earth to dry infinity,
Not looking back, glad to leave man and his array

Of baleful manufactures of neon and concrete
That cover our rich loam, cover it with a crust,
Underneath a smog of methane heat;
Pleased that stenciled on our nose-cone, black and neat,
We have the randy slogan "Pike's Peak or Bust!"

THE TRICK

Let me be open. I know nothing,
Nothing better than love. Not money—
And I love to spend it; not power, no!
Nor food—and I love the taste of honey.

And yet one time just when I started
To make love some whisper in me said
"My God, this is ridiculous" and dimmed
The pyrotechnics of the bed

And made me wonder if love was really
Anything more than a magician's flashy trick.
We glimpse the way it's done—our eye is quick—
And yet God knows it works. It lets the lovers
Turn and share the serenest thought, a platinum
Kind of sharing, not to be begged or bought.

TRIO

Christ, yes. Yet I can defeat the sweetened smile,
The liquid hair, the chromo on the religious wall.
Blood is still blood, wine wine; no rise, no fall.
His worship has the touch of cambric, smell of camomile.
And God Himself? Old Jew with waving beard, costumed by Blake,
Colored by Michelangelo, pomped by the Coptics of the trine.
I can see Him and so see Him small; I can define
His outlines—and my guilt. For Jesus' sake,

Or for His Father's, for the heaven of invention or the hell
I will obey the laws, though halt and lame,
Those Two have made who call the least the most.
But the Third I cannot comprehend. I only know that I inflame
With sheerest flame, hear the universe as a bell,
And throwing back my head must cry "O Holy Ghost!"

TASTE

The old Greeks painted their women cream,
Their heroes tan, with coal-black pubic hair.
On pediment and parthenon they splashed their paint:
They couldn't stand to see the marble bare.

They used sky-blue and a demented red, covering
Venus with everything but stars or stripes,
Then stood back, hands on hips, heads cocked
In pleasure as if listening to Pan's plastic pipes.

Today we see the marble's austere white, the paint
Peeled and the crackery dropped off, and its classic light
Moves us beyond words. And so, I guess, will some
Future, furbelowed race, in satinite

Crouch marveling at the bleached bones of Lichtenstein's
Once feathery, psychedelic nudes or stare
At Yoguchi's creamwalled closures or Ann Turnbull's
Swooping globes of ochred clunch
Forgetful of the garish colors that once were there,
Before having some of us for lunch.

PASSAGE

What have we done to death? I, less American than most,
Still must speak stiffly to say "the body," "the corpse," "the
    remains."
The thought dries my mouth. I jeer at Forest Lawn, detest cosmetic
Youth, and yet if I can I ignore death's awkward bulk.

In the Slovenian village where my uncle's father died
They coffined him and took him out under the pale sky.
The villagers formed a procession two hundred meters long,
Flags first, black-buntinged (no cross—he had left the church).

Then the village band, slow marching to brass and beat,
Then our family carrying cedar wreaths, then the coffin on a cart,
And then the villagers by twos and threes on down the road.
I marched too and dropped my pinch of dust into the grave.

I know that this is better than our thin American way.
And yet . . . I look around me and see forming clouds so dense
That I feel that when our village bears a child we should bring him
In his basket home from the hostel and his mother's side,

Flags draped, brass band at slow march, green wreaths, and
Mourning villagers following him down the single street.

CANTATA FOR COUNCIL FLATS

The very rich live, unlike us, in lodges
Eating their money between folds of bread.
The guineas crumble like digestive biscuits
When sharp white teeth meet meat in Wickhamstead.

O teeth, O teeth, I sing your apotheosis.
You are filled with ivory, elephants, or gold.
Outside the lodge the ice drifts upon the windows
But you never need to chatter with the cold.

The very rich glide encased in blubber.
Great whales, they spout pure ambergris
Which perfumes all the air around them
And makes us think, Will wonders never cease.

Be thankful the rich are still among us.
Their presence though extrinsic purifies the air.
Clerk or char, messenger or mountebank, scholar,
Shoemaker or drab: upon your scarfed knees
Praise God for every pouting millionaire.

What if you have to squat for shillings?
You still are trendy-randy Now
And nightly on Kings Road can wear elf boots
And helmet hair and plaids designed
To let you peacock as the cameras bow.

Stuffed moonlight is exactly what you have, but never mind—
You sing somehow.

THE PLAYGROUND

Carolyn: ten, wide-eyed, still skinny,
Knobby-kneed; can throw a baseball like a boy;
Across the bounded asphalt flats can speed
To greet her father with a raucous joy

And nearly knock him backward; not much
Manners. And I, her father, skinny too,
I should have seen her trumpets and her banners
But my own stiff youth was all I knew.

The brusque March wind has swept the playground bare,
A bareness backed by racks of iron pipes.
I thought too much; I thought that love was fairness,
Seeing only the playground's lines and stripes.

Today the child and man are both grown
Older. Carolyn, I know now what I did wrong:
I should have slung you on my shoulder
Like a sack and marched home to your loud love-song.

Today the playground glistens in the heat
Like foil; lines waver, and the pipes above them.
When you have given me grandchildren to spoil,
I shall. I shall be wise and simply love them.

THE EPITHALAMIUM EXPRESS

White-haired, they look hands folded. They walk by
Short meanders. They ask in Budapest about one
Another's digestion; in Naples they agree to nap. One

Night in Vienna they dare to take the Frivolity Tour,
They sit with the bus load at the godawful nightclub
Eyeing Venus' belly through a glass of tourist champagne.

The hotel whore watches them wanly, declining to think.
Her beads deploy in tremulous amber, far fringing the
Bare Pannonian steppes. Fields wider than Nebraska

Reach past umber to green to ice. Chronos drums with
His eleven fingers till Pan fetches him a rump. The
Bellboy and the gaping chambermaid clutch each other

As if being pulled apart. Ah love, let Artemis celebrate
The morganatic night. Quick into bed before the bus
Comes and the tour director, gray-gloved, beckons with

His polylingual hand. I swear, by black hair and hard
Thigh, that I will never wait but will take my bride
To Bucharest tomorrow. Now, new, we will visit randy

Vienna, playing statue or Rhodomontade, walking naked
Through the Corso
To the fountain
At the height of noon.

MONKSHOOD

Believe me I can tell you the secret.
I have the formula. Read these few lines
And they will make you rich. I guarantee it
Or I provide the analgesics and anodynes.

Next to the canistel and rhubarb you will find
Death camass, in ruddy stalks; hellebore displayed
Flowering in waxen health; mescal spined
But crisp to the canine tooth; grass, blade on blade.

Do you begin to see? Are you already
Taller and glossier than you were before?
Is your look becoming full, steady?
As you advance does someone open up the door?

Certainly, certainly. No need to wink at you
Or dig you in the ribs. You have it now—
I see it in the belladonna stare that you
Direct at me a moment before I bow.

THE BUDAPEST ILLUSION

I lay in the Innsbruck convalescent home,
Leg bloated and painted blue.
The iron fence stood high, dogged at the
Single gate. Persian rugs on my sickroom floor,
On my bed French-embroidered sheets. Nurses
Muttering in motherly German, and a spade-
Bearded doctor of course. But no medicine. No medicine.

The leg bloated bigger till, floating, it
Tugged me upward. I dangled from the ceiling
And spoke in Slavic. The doctor piled his beard.
For me the dogs howled at the single gate. The
Rosy nurses chanted incantations. But I soared

Above the steep roof. Till something sharp sucked
At me. I looked through glimmering eyes and slowly
Saw the leeches. Both black, they swelled with
My dark blood until I thought they would burst
Apart. Doctor, delicately gloved, pulled them

Away as Nurse wrinkled a nose. I sank down among
The embroidered sheets while the leeches floated
Like balloons, back to Budapest, while I stopped
Talking in tongues, while I
Looked thoughtfully
At my no longer levitated leg.

CHRIST CONCEDED TO BE A SOUND WE HEAR

My God, is he still alive?
I thought his museum had burned down years ago.
I thought they had made it into a parking lot
And melted the bronze plaque that once marked the spot
Where he had composed his first concerto.

His books are not even sold
As shadows anymore; you cannot even watch
Him posturing on the high-shouldered, late-night films.
You remind yourself, without novelty, that time overwhelms
Us all and all our work, until you hear a catch

Of song on a hot afternoon,
Mournful, an odd turn of two linked tunes, a wisp of smoke,
And then the old soul stands before you with his bleak recorder
(Just as if he had never been treed for murder)
Or playing his whorehouse piano as if it would never break.

I suppose it proves he is still around.
Even though the asphalt has been rolled flat over his pleasure dome
The spike sticks up through the pavement. The torso of marble,
The flung gesture, the final chapter—these survive the rubble
Of the broken room in the old-people's home.

TO CHARLOTTE

I went to the Rent-a-Word agency, my own
Verbs combed, my blond adjectives slicked back.
I fidgeted through the door—
What an inspiration to tone the pediments
In purple and loft the arabesques!
I left you sitting outside, one slim leg
Leaning out of the door of the get-away car,
Tommy gun cradled on one slim arm.
But for you, I would have bolted.

But then the aisles opened, the vault grew deep,
Gray to black beyond.
Against the gathering gloom the flags!
Ranked row on row, brilliant banners,
Blue, solferino, gold.
I walked beneath them, my neck craning
Till it ached.

Then the altar, heaped with vocabulary; attendants
Slippered and liveried, blazoned with buttons saying
Word. Incense in fluted columns, musk, amber.

Till I heard the horn honk as you pressed it
With gloved, impatient hand; and the motor
Racketed; and you called my name.

ST. CARNIVAL

Step outside, sir, and see the human head.
Most visitors notice the nose first, I suppose;
Who can escape this snuffling beak, now pink, now red,
With its odd flare and its twin holes?

Others are attracted by the teeth,
Shiny white bits of bone that catch and rend,
Or the irised eyes above or the busy chin beneath.
But as I conduct the noted guests around

The head I am always fascinated by the ears.
Grotesque, voluted, pink impossible shells,
They grow even larger with the passing years.
And yet late at night we talk among ourselves

About a handsome profile or a pretty face.
I have composed a prayer! It begins
God give us accustomed heathens grace.

PERSONAL LETTER TO THE EPHESIANS

Delay thine ancient luncheon, Bud—
Let cold meat grow colder still.
And you, my histaminic friend,
Stop your snuffle and attend
While I fill you in with fill.
I have a message for you and Bud
Aimed at enriching your tired blood.

Put your orts on the sacred table.
Slide them there when the Lord's not looking.
He'll never ask for more to eat—
This is merely a god you cheat.
Reject the Lord but savor the cooking:
Deny the myth yet dignify the fable.
And feel as little as you are able.

Who speaks with the voice of the modern churches
To you at noon at the factory gate?
Who dresses the Lamb of God
With a butcher's ruddy cleaver?
Who serves you as you wait
With a wine for slips and lurches
Which tastes of brass and rod
To any true believer?

Who dresses the Lamb of God
With a butcher's cleaver?

DUPLEX

Not much of a war hero but enough,
Barely enough,
To get me buried, free, at
Arlington,
Plus a part-fee for the undertaker
And a folded American
Flag.

All mine if I crave it
And I do.
And later on—did you know this?—
My wife can be buried there too
Free.

And yet there is one small
Hitch, or maybe it isn't. But
Anyway—I didn't know this myself—
What they do at Arlington and
The other veterans' cemeteries is
When your wife dies
Dig open your own grave down to the
Coffin,
Put hers on top of it,
And then fill up the grave again.

My wife and I have been closer than
Most married pairs . . .

I shun all metaphysics,
All metaphors,
And only ask,
Why does the thought shake my bones?

PUNTER'S PEAK

You pole the punt between the Cambridge June
High-banked, leafy, clotted with cream,
And the raw April, sky-studded and shaking.

Knowing that April will never intrude again,
That the Cam's easy, early summer breeze
Will stay steady. You will see the willows

Dance a bit while the other punts pole by,
The one with half a dozen ruddy Cockney boys,
The one with Ron, his girl, and his Mum—

Mum sitting up stiffly, about to pour her tea
And looking dry at the passing punt poled by
A limber girl in her white panties and pink bra.

Along the green edge your father rides the bicycle
Of the mind and frightens water-rats; already hoarse
He shouts "Hard ho! Hard ho!" You think.

The sun slides on, a few greenflies flutter near.
The ducks sail or scold, the swan dabbles.
You pole the punt and never feel it sough

Yet somehow you slope to Grantchester,
To the old vicarage and fakey Rupert Brooke.
You take your tea in the orchard on tabled tin

Tasting each drop, sure that you will seldom
Have another afternoon quite as good as this,
Not even under a Tasmanian moon in camp.

There is no punting back. It only looks downstream.
You hear the rapids' muted roar or see the waters'
Slow collapse. So why not down an ale to the best day
Of your life, at the bump supper your father has biked along?

UNWEATHER

What can you say that is new about
Snow? In this town the soot speckles it in a day,
The sun lowers it and makes it leak away.
And I hate the wind. I can hardly wait for it to go.

Slabdash the politician likes a blowsy
Air. It ruffles his big coat and nudges his fat gut.
His snow is dirty and drab, his Virgin is a slut,
His God a bully beard. And Slabdash grows anywhere.
All I ask is this: Why do I have to want a thing
To be new? Why can't used words work just as well,
Or a stale bed or a dirty altar?
                    Why must the beautiful be true?
It doesn't make any difference if snow won't keep.
It shouldn't bother me.
                    Why can't I sleep?

THE MAGIC WORD

The Atlantic Monthly now flavors its pages with the word "fuck."
James Russell Lowell stands like a pink flamingo,
On one long leg, colored by embarrassment as
    Well as the shrimp he regularly eats.

Oliver Wendell Holmes and the rest of these whiskered New
England worthies look the other way as they dance
Sedately past, legs licking halfway up and arms
    Linked long before prancing was perfected.

And I cannot describe the confusion of the fusty female
Virgins as they hold their pens high—and you know
What those stand for—about to stab their black
    Bombazine bosoms with the selfsame

Instrument that indited their lyrics in the Atlantic. Oh
How proud the neighbors were to know the Maine poetess
Whose "Sand by the Seashore" was accepted, printed,
    And paid for promptly on publication.

The Elders of Corinth turn in their epode to the Trojan Women.
Their joint lamentations startle even the coveys of cod
In the Boston harbor. Through the fog the salutary
    Slambang emerges smelling of elderly fish.

Moreover, the magazine, confident of its rectal correctness,
Rigid in its pride and progress, prints the story of
How DNA was discovered, prints it in language clear
    Only to the professors of chemistry at

Harvard—MIT need not apply—making but a single concession
To the public, which always renews its subscription,
Of putting the story into larger type than usual.
    Moreover, its articles on Viet Nam remain gutsy.

Moreover, its dialogue grows curt. Oh the Atlantic
Monthly is with
It, as it seizes its shaker of Accent, like a shameless
Julia Child, and liberally over the browning pages
    Sprinkles the word "fuck." But I guess
    It is easy once you get used to it.

22

TEATICKET AND THUMPERTOWN

I sing Cape Cod in August—when across the Bay
I can see the houses Hopper painted, tiny geometric forms,
Sharp in the sunlight and yet with an air of storms.

For the weather has beaten the colors, has dulled the rooster-
Red and oyster-white; but the lines of the houses still
Show rectitude. You can hear them saying, Right is right.

The pure cone of the lighthouse seems only a tiny shaft
Tipping the end of the island, striking its small hour.
Into the pure, clear breeze it leans like Pisa's tower.

It knows there is more than August, that howling
Winter waits, to sweep over the shuttered cottages,
To snow the Truro dunes, to ice the Magellan straits.

It needs an idiot to sing the lack of beachwood fires
While eyes water as they watch the icy wind and fail
To see a single mote move on the sandy shires.

And yet my weatherbeaten neighbor tunes his weather-
Beaten voice in bleakest February, standing by the
Stiff cranberry bogs as if his winter were most choice.

I sing Teaticket, Thumpertown, and lucid sun.
He hymns the arctic Cape and an iron house for everyone.

THE FAMILIAR

Neither God nor Plato though bearded and sublime
Could stay her headlong lusty course; it took time.

Time like a great squat cat scratched at her cheek.
Once, resting from her life, she screamed when Tom swept
Onto her naked back; claws clung like a nympholept.
Her fears gathered at her back, stinging and sleek.

She lay on the bed of spice till one huge paw
Turned her over. Behind her eyes, white surged;
Sight washed away till all sense was submerged
Under time, and time was all she saw.

Mist covered her hair and resolved her face;
She stared at the bathroom mirror as if
It could go away. She looked down from the Nauset cliff,
Yearning for the sea below as the safest place,
                    The safest place.

MALEDICTION

The water hurries toward me, whipped by the same
Wind throwing sand onto my face. The sky in its
Folded gray lowers over last Sunday's lace.

The witchgrass bends in wavering clumps, in light-
And dark-green arcs. The smell of salt sweeps by
And the sharp New England smell of sharks.

Everything is arrowed at me. Stumbling, cursing, I
Must quail for shelter by the nearest dune but the
Wind slides down like water, drenching me with hail.

White and chilled I crouch like a motley pigeon,
Feathers ruffled in despite. I crouch day after day
—And each day is worse than any Calvinistic night.

So I curse again and then stir enough to think about
A barricade. I scuttle head down to the nearest sign
—The beach is thick with those that man has made—

To pull it by its spine and plant it by the boat . . .
An hour's work, and I lie warm, cosseted like a
Convert, quite out of the Antinomian storm,

Behind: Bridge Out; World's End; Posted Against the
Sun; Dog; Church Closed; God; Keep Off Everyone.

THE MAGES

I hear the soldiers thrumming on their boxy Aeolian harps.
Fettered eagles scream on the standards. In the bay I see some sharks.
Along the rumpled sand, sweaty in their fiber-foam armor,
The soldiers move, hailing each sunburned farmer.

If salt blows in from the marshes, to crystal on their hand,
Their eyes will blink refraction, turning a bluish bland.
They will march blind over the battens, with just the
Harps to tell us the soldiers are coming for matins.

Eyes shut, they will shoot pointblank at the unseen target:
The child in the yard, the farmer hoeing, the wife at market.
Volley after volley, soft cotton puffs in the sky.
Long after the stumbling soldiers have made their sally

And become black dots on the distant dunes, the down-
Shore wind will waft us the harps' weird Aeolian tunes.
Tomorrow their keening will still be heard. The farmer's
Restless son, dropping his hoe, will suddenly be stirred.

THE WINDOW

My wife asleep, her soft face turned from me,
My children sleeping in their rooms as well,
I get up, drawn to the window, to see what I must see:
Silver, and black and silver. There is almost a silver smell.

The moon on this burnished California hill,
The stars with their sober silver spark.
I know. And the savor of the night through the patch of dill.
If I could drink aromatics or take eucalyptus bark,

If I could drink sense and have its glow to keep,
Or even if I could bathe the folded shapes of words
With any light of mine this once, then I could sleep.
Straining, I stand and can hear no sound, no birds . . .

But all at once there comes the howl of a far-off hound
And all that I want to say is said in that single sound.

The Conjurer's Cloaks

THE WITCHDOOR

The keeper of the Pemmaquid Inn, Tom Potter, turns
Out at five, when the sea is still only a cold glow on
The inlet and hardly a guest is alive.

He walks in flannel so as not to wake his dead,
Starting the endless roll of chores he has envisioned
During his last few minutes in bed.

With pitch he lights the fire beneath the cauldron,
Drops in a few fillets of fenny snake, lights the
Two black candles, and then for the

Black mass frosts a wafered cake. It is now time
For him to lean out the diamond-paned window, throw
Back his head, and whistle a weird rhyme.

Its sound floats over the marshes and the gawky marsh
Hens hear. The lizards leap from their sleeping
Stones, the mewing seagulls swoop near.

A host of Tom's familiars, from land and sea and air,
Draw in for the piquant breakfast they know Tom can
Prepare.

They throng through the single window and gulp or
Sip from the boiling pot. Ravenous, splattered with
Blood soup, they blood the entire spot.

Till Tom nods once and they stream away through the
Window, leaving Tom alone. He takes an enormous
Rag and swipes the pot and stone.

When the first paying guest stumps down the stair
All he smells is savory sausage and eggs frying
As he sees Tom bending there

Over the burnished electric range, dialed like an
Old radio set. Tom looks up, grins a gat-toothed
Grin, and promises him the best breakfast yet.

TRANSPOSITION

In the states of Arkansaw, South Dakota, Mississippi,
Idaho, and Ouisconsin—the blue-bellied, the
Stone-arid, the red-clayed and pecker-wooded—
It is still illegal
For the woman to be on top
During intercourse.
Mention that at your next cocktail or pot party;
It'll bend some minds.
The two street signs glow neon at ten
In the absolutely flat night.
Even the drugstore is shut. At the corner
A cigaret tip glows but only one.
Otherwise, all Midland is coupling.

The beds heave in wavelike ripples along the town.
Springs softly twang to the echoes of other springs.
Only the room above the filling station
Is remarkable.
There the man groans, pressed to the mattress,
"My god, you're smothering me,"
While ruthless Venus wiggles.

But otherwise, over the broad expanse of
Darkened and benighted states
The male mounts.
In Arkansaw and South Dakota he has shucked
His underwear. In Mississippi and Idaho
He drops on his target from the chandelier.
And in Ouisconsin he slides on the
Stockyards like yesterday's greased pig.

Cheerful or baleful, love's tatterdemalions
Punch the Judy of the isotopes. The sand
Ripples in the vast retorts, the desert camels
Nose the tents, the earth heaves over its core of
Fire.

Let it go at that.

THE PLANET

The solid ocean and the liquid land:
On both—free from my cage of ribs, dressed
In my Sunday best—I steadfast stand
Or sailing sing hosannas which call me blest.

Onward the ritual winds, the vestments sway.
Through the church windows the rain shines down
In lucent drops upon the sunny day.
And I—I die indefinitely of brown.

I rise; to ponder puzzles or to peer
At the prettiest girls in church. I sit;
And stare at the blonde one kneeling near.
I kneel; and undress her lovingly bit by bit

Until at last, the benediction done,
I bolt; and see you beckoning in the cosmic sun.

THE SEER

There are holes in the sky, the goat-bearded astronomer
Says, sailing his charts like elegant paper
Airplanes or twirling his astrolabe between his fingers.

Nightly he climbs to a perch in the absolute blue
Armored in his long underwear with the dropseat.
He whistles on his knuckles under the frost.

The tune floats up to Cassiopeia in her chair,
Who hears it and stirs. She looks through the
Holes with her fixed frown, frowning.

There are holes all right, and who do you think
Is sitting at the bottom of the deepest one?
Me, you bloody astronomer, me.

And I have a message for you that you will remember.
I have the words spelled out against the farthest
Reach. They say: Happen, Happen, Happen.
Cassiopeia taught me not to pry.

CONFUSION

Having seen most of my blood spilled on the bathroom
Floor at four o'clock this morning (how well I took it;
No panic) I have come this late afternoon to certain
Conclusions. Verbena is yellow; the smell of blood

Caked in the nostrils is actually something like
Brass—previous poets and old-school novelists
Have not lied to me. The orient rests like a rose
Occiput while across its taut horizon werefolk slink

With a certain style. The Druids hold a final mass
Before turning in their beards and ripping their
Saffron robes into cleaning cloths, not very soft.
High above me hangs a bag of blood, guaranteed to

Sing in concert with mine. Having been stabbed by
Cunning white females I lie open-veined accepting
Drop by drop what seeps into me. In vein and artery
And all parts of that system whose names I do not know

I am new. Without you I would be dead. I thank you
For sharing you with me. I am you, Mrs Rossiter,
Aged 35, hair still blonde, only two small wrinkles
At the corners of your warm mouth, more than if I

Had slept with you and our breathing had crescendoed
Together. Maybe, maybe, I now have more of you than
Mr Rossiter himself, home from the figleaf factory. I have
Been in nooks and crannies that Mr Rossiter would

Never think of. His imagination would boggle at where
In Mrs Rossiter I have been. (But the husband is always
The last to know.) And Mr Rossiter does not even guess.
By god I am going to get well and then it might embarrass

Mrs Rossiter to find where some of her blood will be
Coursing. Or maybe not. Maybe she would be amused.
Anyway, she has brought me back and I love her for it
And there is actually a slant sun outside my hospital

Window and Mrs Rossiter, you had better not come near
My hospital bed or things will happen to our inter-

Chemistries that no courts will ever be able to
Untangle. The courts know nothing closer than

Incest—but Oh Mrs Rossiter, wait till I catch hold of
You.

LOVE CALL

The grass a smoldering red, the trees like cinnamon,
The sky an umber brown.

There lies my Aeolian harp, above the livid sedge,
Set artfully upon the window ledge.

Soft and eerie is the sound which Satan hums,
And through the harp it comes.

This is no blunt god of wind blowing on strings.
This is sin itself that sings,

Vibrating and resonating, shaking the wooden box:
The sound that music mocks:

The melody of an underworld or the song that Circe sang.
No siren's notes can ever hang

In the evening air like this. From house to house a
Keening swells: his widows put on black.
Baleful, bart-bearded, Ulysses has come back.

DOCTOR OF PHILOSOPHY

Explain him—the fly bull never shoots.
Hypothecate your bottomry; cry pax;
Take off your lily gloves, hand up your axe.
Deny that you and I were ever in cahoots.

Who would be fractious, who would dragoon
The lone traveler, cloaked on the hilly hill
Black against the sun, or shoot against his will
Him through the swinging doors of the wood saloon?

Not me. You carry the mail. If it's wrong
You did it, friend. To Athens you brought the owls,
You buttered bacon, you flapped your arms like towels.
You threshed about, kicking gong after gong—after gong.

Oh well. The bell shrills. I negotiate alone
Among the pinchbecks, the fraid holes, the pot-hooks,
Very careful of what I say, citing my source books
But only breathing into the telephone.

THE GNOME

Nine feet below the sea-sand my Uncle Ronald sits,
Hunched in a cave of caverns, turning the tables of
The tides, muttering by starts and fits.

He also waits for little girls who, armed with shovel and pail,
Dig too far in the sodden sand till they reach the
Watery wash and earth's foundations fail.

The girls cry out for their mother as they softly softly sink.
Through the sand, clutching their red tin shovels,
They slide down the abyss to the brink

Just above my Uncle Ronald, who wets his rubbery lips.
The girl's feet drop through his ceiling. Their tiny toes
Show first, then struggling legs, then hips.

Oh hips. When the little girls' guileless mother
Returns in her plummy bathing dress
She will find only a pair of pails and a dimple in
The stretching sand—and perhaps in the air above her
A tiny echo of distress.

THE PETALUMA TRIP

Me, I'm happy enough at the prune-flake factory.
I can walk to work. I can walk to work.
But on a morning like this, in the sun,
I want that Mercury, bad.

I want to be whizzing down the parkway
With the red racing-stripes jetting the dual carburetion.
I want it to be a long trip, so I've fixed up
A clothes rod above the back seat—
Just the way the salesmen fix them.
And on the hangers, sharp-looking
Jackets and slacks.

And I want a red-haired chick, breathing perfume,
Settling next to me, talking in my ear,
Kidding at all the other cars we pass
Especially the mom-and-dad ones
With dad with his hat on.

And on the hangers her dresses too, all short, all snug—
Yellow, blue, orange.
I drive and she nestles close. And the clothes
Sway on the hangers as I round
One smooth curve after another.
And we circle.

Higher and higher, over the clover-leafs,
Way above the lawns on each side of the parkway,
While the soft air intoxicates,
While the sky swirls in coiling rainbows,
While my girl melts into me,
While the Mercury soars along the multi-colored mist—
Till I live and die at the same instant.

PIGEON PIE

Oh I had my fantasies when I worked at Grosvenor Square.
I often imagined the beautiful Slavic spy
To whom I could sell Embassy secrets.
I would have confessed to her all about cultural exchange.
Or American authors.
Fondling my tie, she would have whispered in my ear,
"Tell me, my American, about the secret life
Of Walt Whitman or E A Poe."

Or I would have played and lost the final match at Wimbledon
With great gallantry, while the British galleries,
Who always love a loser better than a winner,
Stamped and shouted
And Princess Margaret wiped a tear from her eye
When I lost the fifth and deciding set.

But my most abiding dream
Was to kick a pigeon on Grosvenor Square.
Fat and pursy, they affronted me enormously with their
Pompous wobble. They came from all over,
Flocking in from Sheffield or from Slough
As well as from the nearby squares.
Fed by idiots, they left only droppings in return.

Yet I never dared to kick one.
There was always somebody who would have seen me.
It would have created an international incident.
I can see the placarded hosts now, chanting,
"Pigeons have Rights like People"
And bashing in the Embassy door.

I never dared . . .
But sometime, flying in on the Jumbo Jet,
I shall sidle to Grosvenor Square, look around swiftly,
Pick the fattest pigeon, snarl at him, "I'll foul your
Footpath for you," then give my sudden kick.

Oh the flock will rocket up, squawking.
All but that pigeon.
It will waddle faster than pigeon ever waddled before,

Holding its wings back tightly over its bruised behind,
Eyes popping, speechless in indignation.
Never again will it drop a stain on my jacket.
Never again will it enjoy spiritual security.
After this it will always look back over its shoulder.

And I shall slip back to New York on the 747,
A relaxed and satisfied man.

THE GUISE

Through the soft panes of window glass bellying
In the bedroom breeze, through the pink-toed bricks,
Through creamy marble, I march and feel
Maligned. I know how I must look and act.
I know I must be designed.

My beard I paste on with some Elmer's Glue
Above, beneath, beyond my fenny nose.
The moustache curls far past my ears and
Redly blooms the rose until my hair smells gingerish.
A cloud surrounds me like a cotton sunset; an oval
Mirror mellows me by its galloon and gimp.

My eyebrows I have cut from coffee fur,
Thick, spongy brown. I stick them on and
Find, not too displeased, that they knit into an
Awesome frown. I look for lips, scuffling
Through my dresser drawer. I find that I
Have only one. I put it on.

My present eyes I am reconciled to keep.
They are by no means patched beyond repair;
They look as searching as they ever did in
My blind man's bluish stare. My wig is rusty raven,
The right bird to be hatted with, its wings
Clasping close to my temples as if
It were still half alive.

Now I am ready to rise and go down the
Rocking stairs, into the unsteady street, where
Among the gorgons, curb angels, amphitrites;
Among the grocers, succubi, and manticores,
Remittance men, diced gypsies, and varnished whores
No one will notice me. Except for you,
Running up, arms out, smiling,
Ordinary and free and true.

THE ARGONAUT

If rain falls on the salt marsh and spots my
Spotty page, if the wind ruffles the curlew's
Plumage and shows my age, if the surf souses
The mild inkberry in sluff,

If the sea water slides down to the center
Of my solitary bowl, swelling over my head
And tossing papers over the edge, if my
Canvas hammock bellies enough

On the tide, having dumped me casually over
The side, then will you rescue me and be
My wife? Will you save me, mouth to
Mouth, for life?

And will you cut my single bean and three
Peas with a knife? Even if my scrabbly
Words are flushed away by the surging
Salt water, even if

I confess in your sandy bed that I already
Have three sons and a grown daughter, even
If I never write another line but only
(Sailor-like) clutch you and clip,

Mounting the moon, muttering in
Your coral ear, "Take
Ship, Take ship"?

OLD ADAM

My love is like the Cape Cod sun, dangerous
Close at hand.
She scorches me if I come too near but otherwise
Is bland.

I breathe faster as I watch her walk. My blood jumps
With each sinuous step she takes:
Her tanned skin flows in rondures but in forms no
Rondure makes.

She glides before me without a stitch on, delighting
My hard Puritan heart.
I cannot see enough of the complex melting of part into
Each smooth part.

I follow her from the sand onto the road. Nothing moves in
The amber heat but us, no people and no cars.
This noon even the churches are close-shuttered just
Like the bars.

Then, then we glimpse the red octagonal sign that warns:
"Drive Slow / Blind Child."
We look at one another. What is the fruit of love? Must
It be good and evil reconciled?

BEGINNINGS

Was the Word.
The first time you touch a woman, the very flesh
In a suave rise of orient sun,
Soft, firm tender curve.
The first time you walk stiffly
Among the temporary dead,
Deaf to their crying or crowing.
Beneath your boot the small bones snap
As they never will again.
The first time, transfixed, you see from far off
The windy plains of Troy, the vast steppes of Astrakhan,
Illimitable snow, and then the mind of God Itself.

Beginnings are good. But terminals? . . .
How do you—forgive me—get rid of a woman?
How do you tell her that,
The curve descending, the lumen gone,
You have finished? Even leaving
A prostitute, do you shake hands and say
God be with you?

And how do you leave Green-Lawn?
The entrance beckons, bold and arched,
The iron grillwork painted gold,
The road gravelled and the pathways plumed.
But you wander bewildered through

The tall stones and low mounds. The embedded lawns
Rise toward the horizon—but no horizon happens.
Look high as you can, there is never an exit marked.
Earth shows no rim; the sky lacks edges.
Panting you sink back to the bottom of
A vast concave. Eternity is a white circle, surely,
Slowly revolving, cooling, chilling.
Yet who can see a conclusion?
Who can see a conclusion?

RX

God watches those that scoff at the old.
He gives them ice-cream cones and
Arthritis.
As they couple in bed, heaving with vigor,
He has the cat jump on them with
A bloody screech. The groin dries
And the erection wilts like
Last week's lily.

Let all those who shoulder the old aside,
Who preen themselves on the brute fact
Of being young,
Let them be taught manners, even wisdom,
By slow pain
And let the bushy boy who laughs the loudest
Stiffen to an arthritic skeleton

Standing permanently cemented
While birds nest in his eyebrows, while
Children chalk graffiti on his rear
And then cavort gleefully away.

THE MINERS OF NEW YORK

At night I watch the miners coming up
From underneath the earth, faces black, eyes glazed,
Swart sweat across their shirts,
Each carrying his lantern and his cup
And his case made from the skin of attachés.

They head for the nearest pub to plug their stills
And jostle each other through the burlap doors.
They gulp a gross and turn
Their orient eye to where, on the high bar stools,
Legs crossed, sit the shiny whores.

The whores smell sweet or musk
Under names like Brenda, Bobbie, or Patrice.
They promise couches deep enough to drown,
Smart girls who in the smoky dusk
Each evening profitably lie down.

The moon walks in the squeak of slates; the
Miners make their love with gathered brow, then grope
Up hill. Above, the pitted night still waits.
They think they hear the thunders of the cataract of hope.
Miners, I spare you hard-breathing sermons on the soul
But you would be better in Denbigh digging coal.

EVERY TIME

I raise the iron bedstead with one hand
And hold it like a torch at sea. My love
Lies on it, dreaming of catnip laced with tea.

To the heavens her smile must seem seraphic
Even if her posture looks slightly lax. She holds
A conversation with the sun, on issues more than facts.

(The sun is seldom good at small talk but can
Make memorable statements in surds.) From time
To time my love translates for me, in words of words,

Though I guess from the sun's mild stare that
Much of the meaning is being undone. I ask it
Politely about God and love and bed, in my pidgin-sun,

Waiting head bent for the relayed answers while
My arm grows tired and begins to ache; if ever
So slightly, the bedstead begins to shake.

My love peers over the edge smiling her wise
Intolerant smile. I tell you, sun, it is hard
To be a man and grows harder all the while.

All she needs to do is to lie there and be polite
But I must raise that bedstead night after night after night.

THE BLACK-FLOWER

Who loving for the first time, thinks about the last?
For me the first was a fevered yesterday
Of drink, cigarets, laughter, and lust;
The woman dark; music beating the floor away.

Tonight, the woman tired, the night warm,
I turn from side to side to ease an ache
Which spreads across my chest, beneath my arm.
Well, let her sleep secure; I am awake.

The stone of rose is painted black; of course;
Who would expect it to be otherwise?
And yet like a fool I twist and curse
As if this pain took me by surprise,

As if I had forgotten, pitch in the sun,
That clenched moment when pleasure and pain are one.

NOCTURNE

Why the hell do you use all that black
In your painting, my neighbor asks across the fence.
I thumb my canvasses, the oboes going slack,
Flutes elegantly wailing, the colors colors of elegance.

Of course the concert stops; the composer done
He wipes his hand upon a greasy rag of fire
Replying flatly that he was only having fun
And who the hell are you, may I inquire?

I crane my neck upon the latest night.
It shapes and opens up into arcades
And avenues and pergolas of light.
My eye, now leading its battalions on, invades
The widening valleys, the martial music bright
With scimitars; and everywhere the neighbors lean on spades.

Epilogue

THE WEATHERMEN

It's happened to you.
It happens to most speakers but especially to poets.
The chairman cradles your elbow as you walk toward
The hall where you will perform.
He looks up at the sky, lowers his voice, and
Explains that this is bad weather for audiences.

You see, the students all have their classes,
The faculty have their eighty-seven committees, and
The townspeople—the only place they go on campus
Is the stadium.

So the two of you scuffle through the yellow leaves,
Stamp over the snow,
Sweat under the hot sun,
Lean into the peltering rain,
Stroll in the idyllic afternoon:
Agreeing all the while that it is
Bad weather for poetry

And if a dozen people turn up
To hear you read your immortal verses,
Be thankful. Your host has had an impossible
Task and he has done the best he could.

Yet you can't help wondering, with one part of
Your mind, as you near Gadarene Hall
(Called by the students Old Gad)
What is good weather for poetry and poets.

Is it balm and babybreath under Tahiti skies,
Is it the Spice Islands or white Tashkent,
Or (God save the tourists) Nassau or Nice?

Or conversely is it under the skudding spray of
The bare Orkneys or behind a black stone at Gander?
Or is it among the amberjacks and dry cascades
Which drift beyond the edge's orient

Like glass needles into mountain vapor?
Or among the smelly, shoving crowds of Chicago
Or the gray ghettos of Third Avenue?

Or is it indeed the weather inside you?
Fickle, unbarometric, affected by sea monsters, blue sails,
And bright angels swarming warm in the bright cold?

Or is it pure essential? Is it ether?

And the chairman holds the door for you
While you walk into the waiting hall.

ACKNOWLEDGEMENTS

Practical Magic contains a fair share of the poetry I've written since *The Man Behind You* appeared in this country. Somewhat less than a third of the poems haven't been published before. The rest have been printed in periodicals and anthologies in America and England. The periodicals I'm reprinting from are: *The American Scholar, The Carleton Miscellany, The Critical Quarterly, Encounter, Expression, The Florida Quarterly, The Hiram Poetry Review, The Hollins Critic, Icarus, John O'London, The Ladies' Home Journal, The Nation, The New Republic, The New Statesman, The Saturday Review, Poetry Karamu, The Southern Poetry Review, The Southern Review, Time and Tide, The Times Literary Supplement, The Transatlantic Review,* and *The Tri-Quarterly.* I'm grateful for permission. The anthologies I'm reprinting from are: *The Honey and the Gall, New Poems* (1963, 1965, 1967), *Poems out of Wisconsin, A Selection of Contemporary Religious Poetry,* and *Today's Poets.* Again, I'm grateful for permission.

For giving me time to write I owe thanks both to the English Department of the University of Maryland and to the University's Graduate School. I wish to acknowledge particularly a summer grant from the Creative and Performing Arts Board and a book-support grant from the General Research Board. And for their interest in my work I feel personally indebted to Professors Morris Freedman and Shirley Kenny, former heads of the English Department; to Dean David Sparks and Acting Dean Robert Menzer of the Graduate School; and to Provost Robert Corrigan of the Arts and Humanities Division—good colleagues all.

C.B.